The Sword and the Cape

Smile

God loves you!

Pauline
BOOKS & MEDIA

The Daughters of St. Paul operate book and media
centers at the following addresses.
Visit, call, or write the one nearest you today,
or find us at www.paulinestore.org.

CALIFORNIA
3908 Sepulveda Blvd, Culver City, CA 90230 — 310-397-8676
3250 Middlefield Road, Menlo Park, CA 94025 — 650-562-7060

FLORIDA
145 SW 107th Avenue, Miami, FL 33174 — 305-559-6715

HAWAII
1143 Bishop Street, Honolulu, HI 96813 — 808-521-2731

ILLINOIS
172 North Michigan Avenue, Chicago, IL 60601 — 312-346-4228

LOUISIANA
4403 Veterans Memorial Blvd, Metairie, LA 70006 — 504-887-7631

MASSACHUSETTS
885 Providence Hwy, Dedham, MA 02026 — 781-326-5385

MISSOURI
9804 Watson Road, St. Louis, MO 63126 — 314-965-3512

NEW YORK
115 E. 29th Street, New York City, NY 10016 — 212-754-1110

SOUTH CAROLINA
243 King Street, Charleston, SC 29401 — 843-577-0175

TEXAS —No book center; for parish exhibits or outreach evangelization,
contact: 210-569-0500 or SanAntonio@paulinemedia.com
or P.O. Box 761416, San Antonio, TX 78245

VIRGINIA
1025 King Street, Alexandria, VA 22314 — 703-549-3806

CANADA
3022 Dufferin Street, Toronto, ON M6B 3T5 — 416-781-9131

The Sword and the Cape

A Tale of Saint Martin of Tours

Written by Pamela Love

Illustrated by Rebecca Sorge

Pauline
BOOKS & MEDIA
Boston

Library of Congress Cataloging-in-Publication Data

Names: Love, Pamela, 1966- author. | Sorge, Rebecca, illustrator.
Title: The sword and the cape : a tale of Saint Martin of Tours / written by Pamela Love ; illustrated by Rebecca Sorge.
Description: Boston, MA : Pauline Books & Media, [2018]
Identifiers: LCCN 2018021025| ISBN 9780819875440 (pbk.) | ISBN 0819875449 (pbk.)
Subjects: LCSH: Martin, Saint, Bishop of Tours, approximately 316-397--Juvenile literature. | Christian saints--France--Tours--Biography--Juvenile literature.
Classification: LCC BR1720.M3 L68 2018 | DDC 270.2092 [B] --dc23
LC record available at https://lccn.loc.gov/2018021025

Design by Mary Joseph Peterson, FSP
Illustrated by Rebecca Sorge

"P" and PAULINE are registered trademarks of the Daughters of St. Paul.

Published by Pauline Books & Media, 50 Saint Paul's Avenue, Boston, MA 02130–3491

Printed in the U.S.A.

TSTC VSAUSAPEOILL6-1310122 7544-9

www.pauline.org

Pauline Books & Media is the publishing house of the Daughters of St. Paul, an international congregation of women religious serving the Church with the communications media.

1 2 3 4 5 6 7 8 9   22 21 20 19 18

For
Chaplains

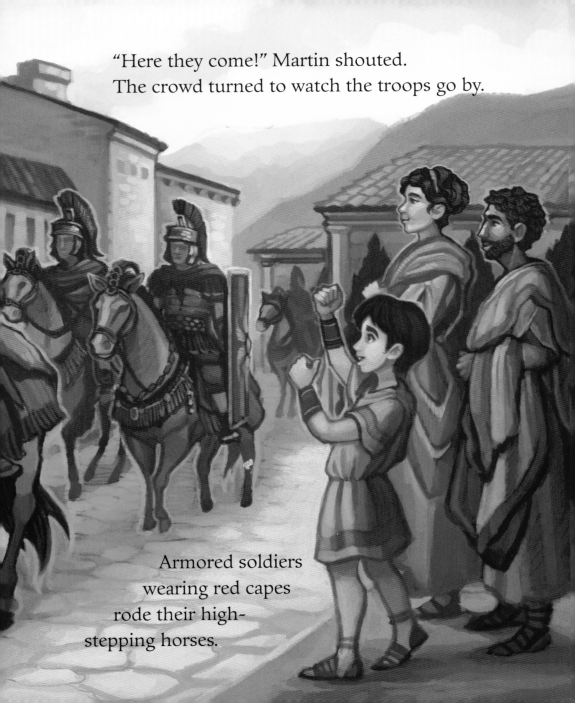

"Here they come!" Martin shouted.
The crowd turned to watch the troops go by.

Armored soldiers
wearing red capes
rode their high-
stepping horses.

It was many centuries ago during the time of the Roman Empire. Martin lived in the city of Ticinum. His father was an officer in the Roman army. Martin and his friends often cheered as Martin's father led the troops through the city. "Someday I'll be just like them," Martin would say. "I can hardly wait."

One day, Martin heard a man preaching on a street corner. "Do you know about Jesus Christ?" he asked the passing crowd. "He is the Son of the one true God. Jesus helped many people. Once a centurion asked Jesus to heal his servant—"

A centurion? Martin wondered. *That's a Roman officer, just like my father.* He stopped to listen to the man in the striped tunic. So did several other people.

"Jesus agreed to go to the officer's house to heal his servant. But the officer insisted Jesus didn't have to go to his house. Just as he commanded his soldiers, Jesus could command someone far away to be cured. Jesus said to the centurion, 'You have great faith. Your servant is now healed.'"

Martin's family was not Christian. They were pagans who believed in the many gods of the Romans. But he was curious about Jesus.

Martin decided to learn more about Christianity. He often visited a church. Sometimes he just listened to the priest teaching about Jesus. Other times Martin asked him questions. Everything he learned about the Christian faith convinced Martin that there is one true God.

On his fifteenth birthday, Martin prayed outside his home. *Lord God, I want to be baptized and be your child. Help me to explain this to Father and Mother.*

Taking a deep breath, Martin went indoors. "Jesus is very different from any god I've ever heard about," he told his parents. "With God the Father and God the Holy Spirit, he is the one true God. I want to be baptized as a Christian."

"A Christian? I thought you wanted to be a soldier like me," his father said. "Looking into this new religion will have to wait. Now that you're fifteen, you must join the army."

Martin couldn't help feeling excited. At last, he would be a soldier! The next day, he enlisted. He learned to march, ride a horse, and use a sword. Like his father, he wore armor and a red cape. His parents were proud of him.

But Martin did not stop thinking about Jesus. Whenever possible, he went to Mass. *I want to be baptized*, he thought, *but am I truly ready?*

Three years passed. Martin was sent far from home to help guard a city called Amiens.

One winter day, Martin rode toward the city gates. Fierce winds blew. Martin pulled his cape more tightly around himself. *I've never felt so cold before,* Martin said to himself. *It's freezing today. Thank you, Lord, for this warm cape.*

As Martin approached the city gates he spotted an old man in rags, shivering. Trying to keep warm, the man sat against the city wall, hugging himself. People hurried past, ignoring him.

Martin frowned. *Someone should help that poor man.*
Then he squirmed in his saddle. He remembered
hearing what Jesus had said about the poor:
"Whatever you do for the least of my brothers, you do
for me."

If I don't help him, I'm not helping Jesus either, Martin realized. *But what can I do? I don't have any money or food in my uniform.*

My uniform . . . Martin had an idea. The crowd
stared in fright as he pulled out his sword.

"That soldier must be very angry," someone
shouted. "Get out of his way, everyone!"

Martin rode up to the old man. Seeing Martin's sword, the poor man trembled, not just from the cold but also with fear. *Why is the soldier so angry with me?* he wondered. *Is he going to hurt me?*

Martin pulled his cape
around and swung his sword.

SLASH!

Martin's cape was now cut in two pieces. He
leaned over and handed the old man half his cape.
"Warm yourself with this," Martin said, smiling.

"Thank you, sir," the old man whispered. Each
man wrapped himself with his half of the red cloth.
The crowd watched, amazed.

Martin rode on. He thought, *If my commander sees me, I'll get in trouble for ruining part of my uniform. But I came here to protect people, and I'm protecting that man from the cold.*

That night Martin tossed and turned in his
sleep. He dreamed of Jesus and angels in heaven. To
Martin's surprise, Christ was wearing half of Martin's
red cape!

Then Jesus turned to his angels and said, "There is
Martin. He isn't yet baptized, but he shared his cape
with me."

At dawn Martin sat up, his heart pounding. "What a dream," he whispered. "I've never had one like it before." He reached for his armor to get dressed.

When he picked up his half-cape, Martin gasped in astonishment. Now it was back to its full length!

That morning Martin dashed to the nearest church. "I want to be baptized today," he told the priest.

The weather was once again freezing, but Martin felt warm inside as the priest poured the cold water over his head.

About

Saint Martin of Tours

In a time when most people never left the town where they grew up, Martin traveled throughout much of modern-day Europe. He was born about three hundred years after Jesus' birth in what is now Hungary. Christianity became legal in the Roman Empire right before Martin's birth, but his parents, like many others, were still pagan—believers in many gods.

When he was little, Martin's father was sent to Ticinum. (That's now the city of Pavia in Italy.) Martin grew up there and became a soldier at age fifteen.

Amiens, where Martin gave away part of his cape, is now in France. A few years after he was baptized, Martin decided to leave the army. "I will be a soldier for Christ," he said.

Martin taught his parents about Jesus, and his mother became a Christian. Later he helped to bring the Gospel message to Germany and to an island in the Adriatic Sea, eventually returning to France. He founded monasteries along the way. Monasteries are places where men, who are called monks, dedicate their lives to working for God and praying. For a time, he was the Bishop of Tours, a city in France. That is why he is called "Saint Martin of Tours." He died in AD 397.

Among other things, Saint Martin is the patron saint of soldiers and horses. Because of the miracle of the cape, he is also the patron saint of tailors and weavers. His feast day is November 11.

The Cape

Martin's cape became an important religious relic. Since Martin became the patron saint of soldiers, armies brought his cape—or, as it was known in Latin, *cappa*—along with them when they traveled. The priest who carried it was called a *cappellanu*—a Latin word that became "chaplain" in English. Today, priests who serve in the armed forces are called chaplains.

When the army was not on the move, they built small churches to hold the cape. They used the Latin word *capella*, which means "little cape," for the little churches. This is the origin of the English word "chapel." Today we call any small church a chapel.

It is believed that Saint Martin's cape was lost in a fire.

Prayer to

Saint Martin of Tours

Saint Martin, you shared what
you had with a stranger in need.
I want to be caring, too.
Please help me to remember
to share with others,
as Jesus wants us to.

After growing up in New Jersey,

Pamela Love

attended Bucknell University. She worked as a teacher and in marketing before turning to writing. She is the author of numerous picture books and has written many stories and poems for children's magazines. Pamela is the author of *Brigid and the Butter: A Legend about Saint Brigid of Ireland* and *Staircase for the Sisters: A Story of Prayer and Saint Joseph*, as well as a contributor to *Family Matters: Thirteen Short Stories*. All are published by Pauline Books & Media. She and her family live in Maryland.

Rebecca Sorge

loves telling stories and drawing pictures, so becoming an illustrator made perfect sense. Rebecca currently lives and works in Utah, where she enjoys creating art for children's books, magazines, posters, cards, and anything else people will let her draw on.

Tales
and
Legends
from

P kids
Pauline

Who are the Daughters of St. Paul?

We are Catholic sisters. Our mission is to be like Saint Paul and tell everyone about Jesus! There are so many ways for people to communicate with each other. We want to use all of them so everyone will know how much God loves us. We do this by printing books (you're holding one!), making radio shows, singing, helping people at our bookstores, using the internet, and in many other ways.

VISIT OUR WEB SITE AT WWW.PAULINE.ORG